Reticulated Python

The World's Longest Snake

by Meish Goldish

Consultant: Raoul Bain
American Museum of Natural History
New York, New York

BEARPORT
PUBLISHING

New York, New York

Credits

Cover, © Jack Milchanowsky/Visuals Unlimited/Getty Images; TOC, © fivespots/Shutterstock; 4, Kathrin Ayer; 4–5, © A & J Visage/Alamy; 6L, © Nick Garbutt/NHPA; 6R, © Joe McDonald/Bruce Coleman Inc.; 7, © Zeynep Mufti/iStockphoto; 8, © Stephen Cooper/Getty Images; 9, © Nick Garbutt/Nature Picture Library; 10, © McDonald Wildlife Photography/Animals Animals Enterprises; 11, © David A. Northcott/Corbis; 12, © Brian P. Kenny/Animals Animals Enterprises; 13, © ANT Photo Library/Photo Researchers, Inc.; 14, © Joe McDonald/DRK Photo; 15, © Joe McDonald/Getty Images/Visuals Unlimited; 16, © Bill Lucey/RainForest Adventures; 17, © Bill Lucey/RainForest Adventures; 18, © James Gerholdt/Peter Arnold Inc.; 19, © BABU/Reuters/Landov; 20–21, © Dr. Meenakshi Harikrishnan/Animals Animals Enterprises; 22L, © Ingo Arndt/Minden Pictures; 22C, © Daryl Balfour/NHPA; 22R, © Bill Love/NHPA; 23TL, © fivespots/Shutterstock; 23TR, © iStockphoto; 23BL, © ANT Photo Library/Photo Researchers, Inc.; 23BR, © Maria Dryfhout/Shutterstock; 23BKG, © Adrian Hillman/Fotolia.

Publisher: Kenn Goin
Senior Editor: Lisa Wiseman
Creative Director: Spencer Brinker
Original Design: Otto Carbajal
Photo Researcher: Picture Perfect Professionals, LLC

Library of Congress Cataloging-in-Publication Data

Goldish, Meish.
 Reticulated python : the world's longest snake / by Meish Goldish.
   p. cm. — (More supersized!)
 Includes bibliographical references and index.
 ISBN-13: 978-1-936087-30-3 (library binding)
 ISBN-10: 1-936087-30-8 (library binding)
 1. Reticulated python—Juvenile literature. I. Title.
 QL666.O63G65 2010
 597.96'78—dc22

                    2009030820

For more information, write to Bearport Publishing Company, Inc., 101 Fifth Avenue, Suite 6R, New York, New York 10003. Printed in the United States of America in North Mankato, Minnesota.

102009
090309CGA

10 9 8 7 6 5 4 3 2 1

Contents

So Long!

The reticulated (ri-TIK-yoo-*lay*-tid) python is the longest snake in the world.

An adult reticulated python can be as long as two cars.

Adult male reticulated pythons can grow to be 33 feet (10 m) long. They can weigh more than 400 pounds (181 kg).

Homes Hot and Wet

Reticulated pythons live in the woods and **rain forests** of Southeast Asia.

They are found in hot, wet places near rivers, lakes, and ponds.

They can also be found crawling through trees and bushes.

Reticulated pythons are excellent swimmers and spend a lot of time in water.

6

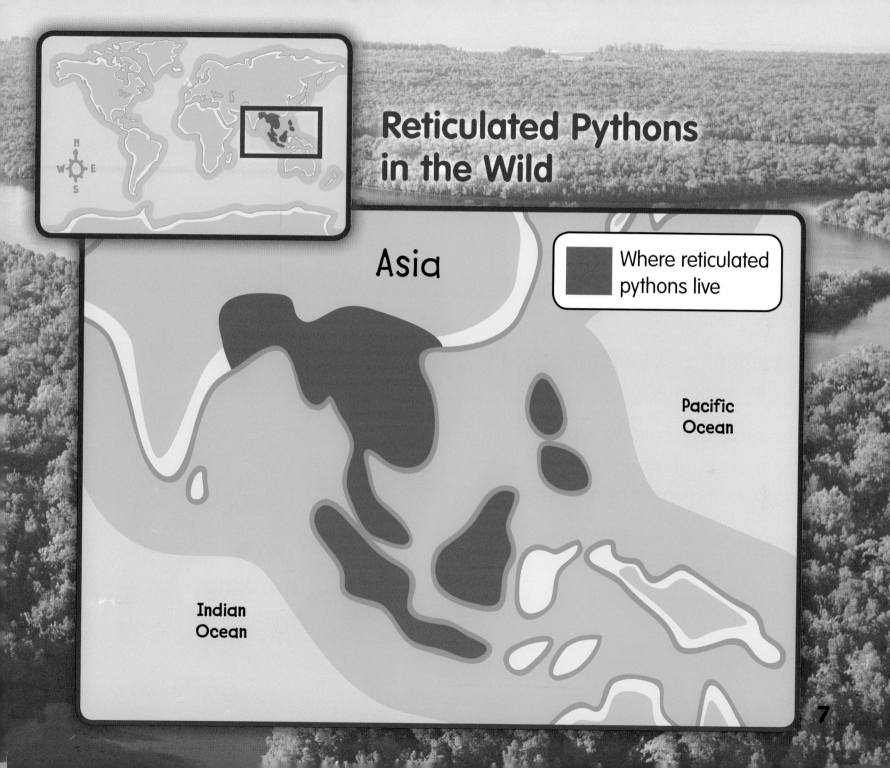

Reticulated Pythons in the Wild

Asia

Where reticulated pythons live

Pacific Ocean

Indian Ocean

Colorful Skin

The skin of a reticulated python is mostly gray or light brown.

It also has small **markings** that can be dark brown, green, yellow, and gold.

Black lines run along the edges of the markings.

The different colors help the python blend in with its surroundings as it hunts for food.

markings

reticulated python

"Reticulated" means net-like and refers to the colorful patterns on the snake.

Finding Food

Reticulated pythons usually hunt for food at night.

Sometimes they wait quietly in trees for **prey** to come by.

When an animal is near, the python senses it by flicking its tongue in and out.

The tongue catches any smells floating in the air.

The python then decides if the smell comes from something good to eat.

Pythons have pits that are located above their lips. These body parts sense heat given off by other animals. The pits help pythons find the exact location of nearby prey.

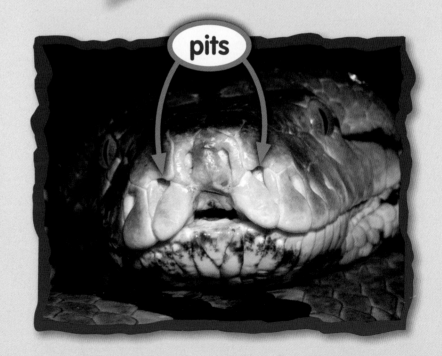

pits

tongue

Bite and Squeeze

After finding prey, the python sneaks up on it.

Then the snake quickly bites the victim with its sharp, curved teeth.

Next, the python wraps itself around the animal and squeezes hard until the victim can't breathe anymore and dies.

The python is now ready to eat.

Unlike many other snakes, pythons don't have **venom** in their bodies to kill victims.

python
squeezing
prey

Meaty Meals

Reticulated pythons are meat-eating animals.

They eat small creatures such as rodents and birds.

They also eat larger animals such as pigs, deer, and sheep.

These snakes can open their mouths very wide in order to swallow large creatures.

Their bodies will stretch to make room for the big meal.

rodent

A reticulated python swallows its prey whole, no matter how big the animal is.

reticulated python swallowing a rodent

15

Python Eggs

Reticulated pythons hatch from eggs.

The female lays between 25 and 100 eggs at a time.

She wraps her body around the eggs to keep them warm.

Then for the next three months, she watches the eggs day and night to keep them safe from enemies such as other snakes.

eggs

A python egg has a soft shell that feels like leather. The egg is a little larger than a chicken egg.

Baby Snakes

Once it's ready to hatch, a baby python uses the sharp tooth in its mouth to cut open its shell.

Then it slides out.

From birth, a baby python can care for itself.

It already knows how to hunt without being taught.

A baby reticulated python is about two to three feet (61 to 91 cm) long at birth.

Growing Up Safe

Baby reticulated pythons are often hunted by other animals such as birds or pigs.

Sometimes crocodiles eat young pythons that swim in rivers.

Once a python grows to be about 10 feet (3 m) long, however, few animals are willing to attack it.

It is then free to grow longer and longer and longer!

Adult reticulated pythons live about 20 to 25 years in the wild.

More Long Snakes

Reticulated pythons are a kind of snake. All snakes belong to a group of animals called reptiles. Reptiles have dry, flat skin covered with scales. They are cold-blooded animals, which means their bodies are as warm or as cold as the places where they live.

Here are three more long snakes.

Green Anaconda

The green anaconda is the world's second-longest snake. It can grow to be almost 30 feet (9 m) long.

African Rock Python

The African rock python can grow to be more than 25 feet (7.6 m) long.

Burmese Python

The Burmese python can grow to be 20 feet (6 m) long.

Reticulated Python:
33 feet/10 m

Green Anaconda:
30 feet/9 m

African Rock Python:
25 feet/7.6 m

Burmese Python:
20 feet/6 m

Glossary

markings
(MARK-ingz)
shapes or designs
that appear on an
animal's skin

rain forests
(RAYN FOR-ists)
warm places
where many trees
grow and lots of
rain falls

prey (PRAY)
animals that are
hunted and eaten
by other animals

venom
(VEN-uhm)
poison from a
snake that is
injected through
hollow fangs

Index

Read More

Doeden, Matt. *Pythons.* Mankato, MN: Capstone (2005).

Schlaepfer, Gloria G. *Pythons and Boas.* London: Franklin Watts (2003).

Weber, Valerie. *Reticulated Pythons.* Milwaukee, WI: Gareth Stevens (2003).

Learn More Online

To learn more about reticulated pythons, visit
www.bearportpublishing.com/MoreSuperSized